Earth laughs in Flowers

ralph waldo emerson

Cooking Up Memories

Amanda Dearing Matti

Order this book online at www.trafford.com
or email orders@trafford.com

Most Trafford titles are also available at major online book retailers.

© Copyright 2011 Amanda Dearing Matti.

All rights reserved. No part of this publication may be reproduced, stored in a retrieval system, or transmitted, in any form or by any means, electronic, mechanical, photocopying, recording, or otherwise, without the written prior permission of the author.

Printed in the United States of America.

ISBN: 978-1-4269-7108-2

Trafford rev. 05/24/2011

 www.trafford.com

North America & international
toll-free: 1 888 232 4444 (USA & Canada)
phone: 250 383 6864 ♦ fax: 812 355 4082

I would like to dedicate this book to my grandmothers (Lady Claire - Mema and Reba - Grandma), my parents (Norma and Peter also known as Gigi and Papa by their grandchildren), my natural mother (Cathy, also known as Nana by her grandchildren), my husband (James), my children, my siblings [David, Shelley (my twin), Jason and Danny] and my friends who were willing to share their favorite recipes with me. My husband has been very loving and patient as this book was created and my family has been VERY supportive through all the rough drafts and the time it took to get to this stage. My husband is my "Quality Assurance Manager" and is always willing to taste my new recipes before anyone else (some are good and some are not so good). I think my love of cooking was inspired by my grandmothers and it has definitely been a learning process. My mother (Cathy) owned two restaurants and is an AWESOME cook herself. She would give me hints whenever I had time to ask questions and we could always count on eating well when we spent time together. I am one of 5 children and my step-mother (Gigi) is an AMAZING woman who raised all 5 of us while going back to school, running her own business, ministering to hundreds with her radio ministry and serving the Lord in all she did. Both Gigi and Papa taught me the value of hard work and dedication and have inspired me to strive to be more than who I am. I know that with God's help, I will always have the strength for anything that may come my way and through his grace, will continue to grow in Him through all of life's trials and tests. I hope you enjoy these recipes and have as much fun as I do when I cook.

John 6:35: "Then Jesus declared, "I am the bread of life. He who comes to me will never go hungry, and he who believes in me will never be thirsty" NIV

Blessings and Peace to you and yours,

Mandy

Through the years I have collected many recipes and had them all stored in a recipe box on my shelf. I have never considered myself an exceptional cook and I didn't want to lose any of the recipe cards I had collected over the years because I need all the help I can get.

Unfortunately, each time I would pull out a recipe card and use it, I would forget to put it back in my box. So, one day, I decided to try to organize them and put them all in one book so that they would be easier to find. Now, after talking to my family and friends and gathering some of our favorite recipes, I am finally finished. Now, I would like to share my recipes with you. I hope you have as much fun as I do when I cook. Please Enjoy and Bon Appetite!

Through the years...

Great Mornings

Favorite Buttermilk Biscuits

- 2 cups of all-purpose flour
- 1 tablespoon of baking powder
- 1/2 teaspoon of baking soda
- 2 teaspoons of sugar
- 1/2 teaspoon of salt
- 1/2 teaspoon of cream of tarter
- 1/2 cup shortening
- 3/4 cup of buttermilk

Combine the dry ingredients, mixing well. "Cut in" the shortening until the mixture looks a little 'crumbly'. Then add the buttermilk and stir together until blended. Turn the dough out onto a lightly floured surface and knead about 10 times. Then you can roll the dough out and cut your biscuits with a biscuit cutter or an inverted glass (that's what I use- it works just as well). Place the biscuits on a lightly greased cookie sheet and bake at 350 degrees for about 10 minutes or until golden brown. Now to make it complete, you need to slather them up with butter, jelly, jam, honey, whatever, and enjoy! If this is a little too much work, then you could also just go for the Bisquick mix. It's easier because it's already pre-measured for you. They're both yummy!

From Scratch...

Jason's Sausage & Cheese Biscuits

- 1/2 pound of sausage (cooked and drained)
- 1/2 pound of grated sharp cheddar cheese
- 1 and 1/2 cups of Bisquick (everything is pre-measured and it makes my life a lot easier)
- 1/3 cup of water

How easy can it get?

All you do is mix the ingredients together, roll out your dough and cut out your rounds. (You can also just spoon out the dough out onto your greased cookie sheet) Then, bake them at 400 degrees for 12-15 minutes. That's it.

You can use your imagination and do what ever you want with this recipe. Add 1 teaspoon of garlic with the cheese (like Red Lobster), or you could add spinach with the cheese. For a sweet flavor, add dried fruit and nuts instead. Do whatever. Have fun with it... YUMMY!

Thanks Jay Bird!

Spinach Quiche

- 4 eggs (slightly beaten)
- 1 and 1/2 cups of milk
- 1 cup shredded / grated Swiss Cheese - or cheddar (You can use whatever cheese you like - just use lots of it - yum!)
- 1 package of Vegetable Soup Mix (any brand will work - but if you have a favorite, go for it!)
- 1 - 10oz package of frozen spinach (thawed and drained)
- salt and pepper to taste

In a large bowl, combine the eggs, cheese, soup mix, milk, and spinach. Then pour into a 9 inch pie crust. A pie crust from the supermarket is perfect for this recipe. Bake at 375 degrees for 1 hour or until a knife inserted in the center comes out clean. Serves 4-6. This is great for parties, because you can make it the night before and just warm it up before the party.

Real Men Do Eat Quiche!

Nana Matti's Cheesy Spinach Bake

- 15 ounces of spinach
- 4 eggs (beaten)
- 1 cup of milk
- 1 cup of shredded Swiss cheese
- 1 cup of cubed white bread
- 1/2 cup green onions / chives
- 1/4 cup Parmesan cheese

Place the bread cubes in a 9 x 11 greased baking dish. Mix the other ingredients together and pour over the top of the bread cubes. Bake at 375 degrees for 25 -30 minutes. I have the philosophy that you can NEVER have too much cheese! So, I always add a little more cheese on top.

Veggies for breakfast!

My Favorite Easy Breakfast Casserole

- 1 bag of frozen "Tater Tots" (or hash browns)
- 5 eggs (lightly beaten)
- 3/4 cup milk
- 3 cups of sharp cheddar cheese (save some for the top)
- 1 pound of breakfast sausage or hamburger (browned and drained)
- 1/4 cup chopped Vidalia Onion
- 1/2 cup of chopped red, yellow, or green peppers (optional) - James doesn't like green peppers

Place the potatoes in a 9 x 11 baking dish and mix the remaining ingredients together and pour over the potatoes. Bake at 400 degrees or until the center is firm and a knife stuck in the center comes out clean. Of course, save some of the cheese to sprinkle on top and then bake it for an additional 10 minutes or so until the cheese is nice and gooey! All your favorite breakfast foods in one dish! Life can't get any better than this!

Tater Tots Rule!

Christmas Morning Strata

- 1 pound of ground pork sausage
- 2 teaspoons of yellow mustard
- 6 slices of bread (white, wheat, pumpernickel, whatever you have - remove the crusts)
- 2 cups of shredded Swiss or Cheddar cheese
- 1 and 1/2 cups of milk or heavy cream
- 3 large eggs (beaten)
- 1/2 teaspoon of Worcestershire sauce
- 1/8 teaspoon of salt, pepper, and nutmeg

First of all you will need to brown the sausage and drain off the grease. Now add in the mustard. OK, next, lay the bread in a greased baking dish and top with the sausage mixture. Add the cheese on top. Combine the milk and remaining 5 ingredients in another bowl and then pour it over the other ingredients in the dish. Bake uncovered at 350 degrees for 50-60 minutes or until set. This is great for Christmas morning, because while we everyone goes through their stockings, the strata can bake. Then everyone can take a break and enjoy a nice hearty breakfast. Merry Christmas!

Dee - lish !!

Easy Eggs Benedict

- 1 English Muffin (sliced in half)
- 1 slice Canadian Bacon
- 1 poached egg (I'll explain how to do it below)

Toast your English Muffin, place the Canadian Bacon on top. Now, for the poached egg... How do you poach an egg? Well, it is easier than you might think. First, heat a pot of water to boiling, then reduce to a slight simmer (we don't want egg drop soup here). Crack your eggs into a small custard dish (not directly into the pot. Carefully slip the egg into the simmering water and cook it about 8 minutes (or until the whites and yolk is firm and not runny). Then remove the egg with a slotted spoon and place it on your Canadian Bacon. Now for the Hollandaise Sauce This will either make the recipe or kill it. When it is done right, it is delicious! You will need:

- 3 egg yolks
- 1 tablespoon of lemon juice
- 1/2 cup (1 stick) of butter not melted

Stir the egg yolks and lemon juice vigorously. Add 1/4 cup of the butter. Heat over *low heat* stirring constantly with a wire whisk until the butter is melted. Then, add the remaining 1/4 cup of butter and continue to stir vigorously until the butter is melted and the sauce has thickened up a bit. Make sure that the butter melts slowly so that the eggs can cook but not curdle.

It's easier than you think...

Mandy's Granola

- 5 cups of oats (the old fashion kind - not instant)
- 1 cup of nuts (Mom likes pecans -- I like almonds)
- 1 - 3.75 ounce bag of sunflower seeds (I like Planters)
- 1 cup instant dry milk powder (for more protein)
- 1 cup of wheat germ
- 1 cup of Grape Nuts Cereal
- 1 cup oil (I use vegetable oil)
- 1 cup of honey
- 1 cup of brown sugar

Combine all the dry ingredients first. Mix it together well and make sure that the brown sugar clumps are gone. Then add the oil and honey. Stir REALLY well and spread the mixture on a cookie sheet or shallow dish. Bake at 300 degrees for about 45-50 minutes or until golden brown. Pour the granola out on wax paper over a cake rack (or 2). It will crisp up as it cools. Dad would eat this on top of his cereal or straight up. Mom prefers it straight up. It is a yummy snack that will help keep you going through the day. To kick it up a notch, you could add raisins, other dried fruit, or mini - chocolate chips. But then I guess it wouldn't be that healthy any more huh? Oh well, ENJOY!

Papa's & Gigi's Favorite!

Shelley's Breakfast Strata

- 1 pound of ground sausage
- 1 cup of sliced button mushrooms
- 1/2 cup of chives
- 2 cups shredded cheddar cheese
- 1 dozen eggs (Yep...12...trust me)

Brown the sausage and drain. Then, in a casserole dish, layer each of the ingredients. Start with Sausage, mushrooms, onions, and cheese. Repeat until you either run out of stuff or run out of room. Scramble your kazillion eggs and pour over the entire strata layers. Bake at 350 degrees for 35-40 minutes. Let it stand for 10 minutes and enjoy!

** You can also add spinach and artichokes, use your imagination...You can add different seasonings (ie. add Italian seasonings for an Italian flair. Or add salsa for a Mexican flavor. Whatever... Use your imagination and have fun with it.

Thanks Sis!

The best and most *Beautiful* things in the world cannot be *Seen* or even touched – they must be *Felt* with the *Heart*.

helen keller

Mema's Breakfast Scones

- 1/3 cup margarine
- 1 and 3/4 cup of all purpose, self rising flour
- 4 tablespoons of sugar
- 2 eggs (beaten) - save some for the egg wash
- 1/2 cup raisins or any dried fruit that you'd like (cranberries, blueberries, and raisins are my favorites)
- 1/4 cup of milk
- 1 teaspoon of cinnamon

Pre-heat your oven to 350 degrees. "Cut" the margarine into the flour until it looks like a crumb topping. Add one egg, the sugar, the cinnamon, and the dried fruit. Add the milk slowly. Once mixed together and the dough pulls away from the side of the bowl, dump it out and "knead" it until it comes together (about 10 times). Now, roll it out to about 3/4 - 1 inch thick. To cut out the rounds, you can use a biscuit cutter or a small inverted glass. If you'd like to go traditional, cut them into triangles with a knife. Place them on your baking sheet and use the remaining egg to "paint" an egg wash on top. Then you can sprinkle some additional coarse sugar on top and bake 15 - 20 minutes or until golden brown.

Thank you Mema! I love you!

Fun Flapjacks

You could measure out flour, baking soda and salt, but life is too short, so I use Buisquick Pancake mix. I just add some extras to make my pancakes extra yummy.

- Pancake mix (follow the box directions)
- 2 teaspoons vanilla extract (butterscotch, almond, or butter pecan is good too - you can add any flavor you want)
- 1 teaspoon of cinnamon
- 1 teaspoon of nutmeg
- Once you pour the batter on your griddle, you can add fresh fruit, nuts, or chocolate chips. (James loves fresh Blueberries!)

Be careful and make sure your griddle is not too hot. If a drop of water 'dances' on the skillet, then it's ready - if a drop of water screams at you then evaporates in about a second, your griddle is too hot! Turn it down! Pour the batter on to the warm/hot skillet. When air bubbles form around the edges, but do not fill in, then it is time to flip. When both sides are lightly brown you're ready to eat!

Southern for "Pancakes"!

The Perfect French Toast

French Toast in itself is pretty easy, but James likes a few extras which gives our French Toast a little extra punch. Here's my recipe for James' favorite French Toast.

- Bread (duh) - I like to use raisin bread but James likes white bread.
- 2 eggs - or more depending on how many pieces of French Toast you are making.
- 2 tablespoons of milk
- 1 teaspoon of vanilla extract
- 1/2 teaspoon of cinnamon (optional)
- 1/2 teaspoon of nutmeg (optional)

Mix all the ingredients in a shallow dish. Dip (not drown) your bread in the mixture and brown on both sides in a skillet over medium with a little bit of oil to keep it from sticking. Make sure your pan isn't too hot. The eggs can burn, so be patient. I promise it is worth it! You can keep the pieces fresh by putting them in a 200 degree oven until the rest of breakfast is ready. (In our house, breakfast usually includes the French Toast plus eggs, bacon, and home fries). YUMMY!

Pancake and Waffle Fruit Toppers

I like to use apples or pears for this one, but you could use almost any fruit you want. You can also use this recipe for toppings on Chicken or Pork recipes. This could also be a side dish, just slice the apples or pears instead of dicing them and try not to stir it to roughly to keep the fruit pieces whole.

- 4 Granny Smith apples-peeled and diced (you could use basically any apple you'd like, but I like the tangy and tart Granny Smith).
- 1/2 cup of raisins (or 'craisins' if you'd like)
- 1 cup of sugar
- 1/2 teaspoon of lemon juice
- 2 teaspoons of vanilla extract
- 1 teaspoon of cinnamon
- 1 teaspoon of nutmeg or 'all spice'.

Mix everything together and simmer (don't boil)- Just simmer for about 30 minutes until it reduces to a nice thick syrup. If you are using this recipe for a side dish (i.e. stewed apples), then just simmer the fruit until it is tender. You don't want it mushy. Dee-lish!!

Starters

The Story of Mema's Deviled Eggs

Christmas Day was (and still is) a big thing for our family. Everyone would anxiously wait for Mema to arrive at mom and dad's house because she had her famous Deviled Eggs! One Christmas, Mema gave me her deviled egg recipe and her deviled egg platter. From that moment on, it was my job to make the deviled eggs. To keep the tradition going, I will usually bring Deviled Eggs to every family function. I come from a big family, so I always have to make lots and lots of deviled eggs. They really are the best deviled eggs in the world and my family can't get enough of them. How do I know this? you ask..... because no matter how many I make, we always run out! It's all because of Mema's "secret ingredient".

Mema's Deviled Eggs (Continued)

- 24 boiled eggs (I told you I had to make a lot)
- 1 cup of Miracle Whip (not real Mayonnaise)
- 2 tablespoons of yellow mustard
- 3-4 tablespoons of sweet pickle relish (to taste)
- 1 teaspoon of salt and pepper (to taste)
- 1-2 tablespoons of deviled ham (Yep. Deviled Ham... this is the secret ingredient- I mean, what could be better than ham and eggs together in the same dish?) It just WORKS! Trust me!

Slice the boiled eggs in half lengthwise and scoop out the yolks into a bowl. Smash up the yolks and mix with the remaining ingredients. Then spoon the mixture back into the empty egg shells. Mema would top them with pimento pieces or finely sliced green olives with pimento. It would add a pop of color and a pinch of extra flavor. Deelish!!

Sweet and Tangy Meatballs

- 1 pound of ground beef (I like ground chuck - it has a higher fat content, but that means that it has more flavor too).
- 1 sleeve of Ritz crackers
- 1 teaspoon of salt
- 1 teaspoon of pepper
- 1 egg
- 1 bottle of Bar-B-Que sauce (I like Bull's Eye)
- 1 can of crushed pineapple

Take your thawed hamburger and mix in the crushed Ritz crackers, salt and pepper and the egg. To really get everything mixed together well, get messy and use your hands. Form the hamburger into 1 inch balls and lay them out on a cookie sheet. Bake them at 350 degrees for about 30 - 45 minutes. Now, take them and place them in a crock pot or large serving dish. Mix your Bar-B-Que sauce and pineapple together and pour over the meatballs. If you're not using a crock pot, then warm the sauce before pouring it over the meatballs. Have your guests self-serve with toothpicks.

Goodness Gracious, Great Balls of Fire!

Traditional Swedish Meatballs

- 1 pound each of ground chuck and ground pork
- 1 egg
- 1/4 cup heavy cream
- 1/4 cup milk
- 1 teaspoon of All Spice and Nutmeg
- 1 small red onion (minced)
- 2-3 cups of bread crumbs

Mix all the above ingredients together. Add the bread crumbs together little by little. You want the mixture to be a little 'wet'. Now, use an large melon scoop to scoop out some of the mixture and roll it into balls. Brown them in a skillet with about 2 tablespoons of oil. Now, it's time to make the sauce. Here we go.... you will need:

- 1/2 stick of butter
- 1 small red onion (diced)
- salt and pepper (to taste)
- 1 small can of beef broth
- 1/4 cup whipping cream
- 2 tablespoons of red currant jelly (trust me)

Mix the first 3 ingredients and sauté until the onions are translucent. Then add the broth and bring to a boil. Now, add the whipping cream and currant jelly. Simmer for about 15 minutes and then pour over the meatballs and simmer until ready to serve.

Dee-lish!!

Mandy's Italian Meatballs

- 2 pounds of ground beef
- 1 cup of crushed Italian flavored Ritz crackers
- 1 egg
- 1 tablespoon of Worcestershire sauce
- 1 teaspoon of garlic powder
- 1 teaspoon of onion powder

Easy, Easy, Easy...

Mix all the above ingredients together. Make 1-inch balls and place them on a cookie sheet. Bake at 350 degrees for 30-45 minutes.

Now you can either mix them with tomato sauce and your favorite pasta, or serve 'em up by themselves with B-B-Q sauce or a tangy Sweet and Sour sauce (Honey, Soy Sauce, diced onions, Minced Garlic, and a splash Sesame Seed Oil). Either way. They are very tasty. Enjoy!

Serve 'em up with marinara!

Growing up, whenever mom would have a party, we were always in for a treat. Mom would make her Melba Toast pizza poppers and we would always get in trouble for eating them before the guests arrived. But they were sooooo good and each pizza popper was the perfect 'bite-sized' snack. YUM!! Sorry mom!

Mom's Easy Melba Toast Pizza Poppers

- Melba Toast Rounds (1 or 2 boxes - it depends on how many guests you have - or how hungry the kids are...)
- Pre-made Pizza Sauce (any brand) - Mom liked Ragu.
- Pepperoni slices
- Shredded Mozzarella Cheese

Just lay out the melba rounds on a cookie sheet, add about a teaspoon of sauce, top with a single pepperoni (they are about the same size - how convenient!). Then top with the cheese and bake at 350 degrees for about 5 minutes. Remember to save some for your guests. They really are the perfect bite-sized snack!

Time for a party?

Mom's Shrimp Mousse
(AKA: "Leroy!")

- 1 - 8oz package of cream cheese
- 1 Can of Campbell's Tomato Soup
- 1 and 1/2 boxes of KNOX gelatin
- 1 bell pepper (finely chopped)
- 1 stalk of celery (finely chopped)
- 1 medium onion (finely chopped)
- 1 can of small shrimp
- 1 cup of mayonnaise

Heat the cream cheese and tomato soup in a double boiler. Dissolve the gelatin in 1/2 cup water. Finely chop the vegetables. Beat the soup with mixer until creamy. Add the gelatin. Beat again. Add mayonnaise. Beat again. Fold in vegetables and shrimp. Grease your mold (Pam works well). Pour mixture into the mold and chill until it is set. (a couple of hours).

When "Leroy" is ready to be served, simply invert the mold on to a platter and serve with Ritz crackers. Leroy may need a little coaxing out of the mold, so you might need to take a butter knife and go around the edges to help him out of the mold.

Finally! The secret is out!

Chick on a Stick (I mean chicken! Keep it clean guys!)

This is a fun, versatile and easy appetizer. Just soak your skewers in water, put your chicken on the skewers, and have some fun. It's up to you. You can grill 'em, sauté 'em, broil 'em, or bake 'em. Add your own marinade or seasonings and enjoy.

Honey Glazed Chicken Kabobs

- Cubed Chicken pieces
- 1/4 cup vegetable oil, honey and soy sauce
- 1/4 teaspoon ground black pepper
- 1 clove garlic (minced)
- 1/2 small onion (roughly cut into 1 inch pieces)
- 1/2 red bell pepper (roughly cut into 1 inch pieces)

Mix together the oil, honey, soy sauce, pepper and garlic. Marinate your chicken overnight and then skewer the chicken and veggies when you're ready to grill. Grill 'em up, bake 'em, sauté 'em, broil 'em, whatever you want. Now, ring the bell. It's time to eat!!

Kabobs!

More Kabob Recipes...

Hawaiian Teriyaki Kabob Marinade
- cubed chicken (2 pounds - cut in bite sized pieces)
- 1 can of pineapple chunks
- teriyaki glaze (Honey, soy sauce, 1 tsp minced ginger)

Mango Chicken Kabob Marinade
- 1/4 cup olive oil
- 2 teaspoons minced fresh ginger root
- 1 teaspoon lemon juice and orange juice
- 1 teaspoon brown sugar and white sugar
- 3 mangos - peeled, seeded, and diced (save 2 to serve over rice with the kabobs after they are done).

Basic Beef Kabobs
- Beef cubes
- cherry or grape tomatoes
- Bell peppers (all colors)
- Pearl Onions (the big ones)
- Salt and Pepper (to taste)

Basic Shrimp Kabobs
- Shrimp (pealed and de-veined) - you can leave the tails on
- Pineapple cubes
- Grape / Cherry tomatoes
- Salt and Pepper - or seafood seasoning.

Pigs in a Blanket (The easiest appetizer of all time!)

- 1 package of Hillshire Farm Lil' Smokies
- 1 can of Pillsbury Croissant Rolls

This is the easiest appetizer of ALL TIME. Most people have forgotten how easy it is, but every time Shelley makes them, they are always the first thing to go. Just wrap the frank in a croissant roll and bake per the directions on the can. You can also use the pre-made pie crusts cut into strips. Whatever works for you. You can sprinkle a little cheese on top to add another layer of flavor. Either way, these are sure to be a hit at any get together.

Naked Sweet and Tangy Piggies

- 2 packages of Hillshire Farm Lil' Smokies
- 1 bottle of your favorite Bar-B-Que sauce
- 1 can of pineapple chunks (drained)

If the first was the easiest, this one ranks a close second. Just put everything in a crock pot until heated through and serve. This recipe also works with meatballs. Just remind your guests to get a new toothpick each time they come back for another bite. No double dipping allowed!

Party Fares...

Tangy Buffalo Wings

- 1 small onion (finely chopped / diced)
- 2 cloves of garlic (minced)
- 1/2 lemon
- 8 oz of tomato sauce
- 1/4 cup Tabasco sauce or Texas Pete hot sauce.
- 1/2 teaspoon of salt
- 3 pounds of chicken drummies and wings (separated at the joint)
- Peanut oil (to deep fry them) (375 degrees)

Buffalo Sauce: Chop/dice the onion and cook over medium heat until transparent. If the edges of the onions start to brown, turn down the heat. Add in the garlic, the juice from the lemon, the tomato sauce and Tabasco sauce. Simmer until you are ready to coat the wings.

The wings: For this recipe, the wings are not battered. You can either bake the plain wings at 375 degrees for 20-30 minutes or deep fry them for about 8 minutes in the peanut oil. When the wings are cooked, simply toss them with the sauce and serve with celery and blue cheese dressing.

Papa's Favorite Coconut Shrimp

- 1 pound of large peeled and de-veined shrimp
- 3/4 cup biscuit mix (I like Bisquick)
- 1 tablespoon of sugar
- 3/4 cup of beer (you can drink the rest)
- 3/4 cup of flour
- 2 cups coconut flakes
- oil (peanut oil works well)

Heat your oil to 350 degrees. Combine the biscuit mix, sugar and beer and stir until smooth. Peel and de-vein your shrimp (leaving the tails on). Then, coat the shrimp with the flour and dip into the beer batter. Gently roll the coated shrimp in the coconut and carefully drop into the heated oil. Be Careful!! Drop the shrimp in one at a time and drop them 'away from you'. You can usually cook 3-4 shrimp at a time depending on the size of your pot. You don't want the temperature to drop too much by adding too many shrimp. The shrimp will cook in about 2-3 minutes. Let the cooked shrimp drain on paper towels and serve immediately with a dipping sauce made with crushed pineapple and sour cream.

Seafood Snacks!

Sweet Cream Cheese Spread

- 16oz of softened cream cheese (2 pkgs)
- 1/4 cup orange juice
- 1 - 8oz can of crushed pineapple
- 1 - 3.5 oz package of instant vanilla pudding
- 1/2 teaspoon cinnamon

Just mix together, chill, and serve. Deelish!

Ham Spread

- 8 ounces sour cream
- 8 ounces of softened cream cheese
- 2 - 8 ounce cans of chunk ham
- 1 small minced onion (or finely diced)
- 1/4 teaspoon of dried mustard
- 1 teaspoon of Worcestershire sauce
- 1/4 cup real mayo (not Miracle Whip)

Just mix all the ingredients in a food processor, mold into a ball, chill for about 1 hour and serve with crackers or pita chips. You could do both of these recipes for any occasion.

YUMMY!

Spread it on thick!

Vicki's Mexican Fiesta Dip

- 1 cup mayonnaise
- 1 cup sour cream
- 1/4 teaspoon of onion powder
- 1/2 cup of shredded cheddar cheese
- 2 tablespoons of your favorite salsa
- salt and pepper to taste

Mix the above ingredients, chill and serve with tortilla chips.

Perfect Pesto

- 1 cup of finely chopped basil leaves
- 1 clove of garlic (minced)
- 1/2 cup olive oil
- 1/3 cup of pine nuts (lightly toasted)
- 1/4 teaspoon of salt and pepper (to taste)
- 1/2 cup grated parmesan cheese

Combine the garlic and oil in a food processor (slowly drizzle in the oil). Add the basil and pine nuts and process until the mixture is smooth. Add the remaining ingredients and process until well blended. Chill and serve with diced tomatoes on bruchetta or serve with pieces of Italian bread as a dipping sauce. You can also toss this with hot pasta, stir it into vegetable soup, mix it into tuna salad, or spread it over chicken before grilling. Just have fun with it.

Thanks Vicki!!

Crab / Seafood Dip

- 8oz softened cream cheese
- 1/3 cup of mayonnaise (not Miracle Whip)
- 1/2 teaspoon horseradish (optional)
- 8oz crab meat
- 2 tablespoons finely chopped onion
- 1/4 teaspoon of minced garlic

Preheat your oven to 350 degrees. Mix all the ingredients together in a bowl. Place in a small baking dish. Bake at 350 degrees for 15-20 minutes and serve hot or cold with crackers. Shelley and I used this one when we were asked to do parties for New Grace Church. If you don't want to serve it hot, just let it cool or chill it in the fridge and serve it cold. Either way, it is dee-lish!

Keep in mind that this recipe can also be changed for those who would rather use lobster, tuna, salmon, or (for those of us who are allergic to seafood) you can also use chicken. But if you use chicken, don't add the horseradish. YIKES!

Great served on crackers!

Easy and Quick 7-Layer Mexican Dip

- 1 can refried beans
- 1 pound hamburger meat
- 2 packages of taco seasoning
- 1/2 cup chopped scallions
- 2 cups sour cream
- 2 cups grated sharp cheddar cheese
- shredded lettuce
- diced tomatoes
- 1 jar of your favorite Salsa

Brown the ground beef and add 2 packages of you favorite taco seasoning. Now, begin layering. Start with the refried beans on the bottom of your dish, then add your hamburger meat, then add the scallions, then add the sour cream, and then, add the cheese. Now you can add lettuce, tomatoes, and more cheese on top with the salsa. Serve chilled with tortilla chips. Yummy!

You could also make this a 5-layer dip by removing the lettuce and tomatoes. Just stop when you get to the cheese. Serve it hot by baking it at 350 degrees until the cheese is all melty and gooey. I like it hot and cheesy, so I usually don't add the lettuce and tomatoes. Sorry...

Time for a fiesta!!

Elegant and Delicious!

Serve with crackers or apple wedges

Almond-Raspberry Brie

- 1 round of Brie (12 ounces)
- 2 tablespoons of seedless raspberry jam
- 2 teaspoons of brown sugar
- 1/8 cup of sliced almonds
- 2 tablespoons of honey
- 1 pre-made pie crust round

This recipe is super easy! All you do is slice the Brie in half horizontally (leave the hard casing on - you can eat it). Then spread the jam on the bottom half of the brie. Leave about an inch around the edge. Place the top half back on. Sprinkle with the almonds and brown sugar. Gently wrap with the pre-made pie crust and bake at 350 degrees until the crust is golden brown (usually between 7 and 10 minutes). Drizzle on the honey and serve warm with apple wedges or ginger snaps. You can basically do anything with this. You can go sweet (with strawberries, cinnamon and sugar, orange marmalade, use anything) or savory (garlic and parmesan cheese or roasted red peppers and olives). Use your imagination and have fun with it.

Elegant party dishes...

Easy Cheese Fondue

- 2 cups shredded Swiss Cheese
- 2 cups shredded / grated Gruyere cheese
- 2 tablespoons of all-purpose Flour
- 1 clove of garlic cut in half
- 1 cup and 3 tablespoons of dry white wine (don't worry, the alcohol will cook out)
- 1 tablespoon of lemon juice
- stuff to dip (bread, veggies, fruit, etc.)

Place the cheese and flour in a zip-lock bag and shake until the cheese is coated in the flour. Rub the bottom of the pot with the garlic cloves. Now add the cup of wine and set on low hear until bubbles begin to rise to the surface (do not boil!). Now stir in the lemon juice. Gradually add the cheese about 1/2 cup at a time and wait until the cheese is completely melted before adding the next batch. Stir it constantly over low heat. Then add the remaining 3 tablespoons of wine. It should be nice and creamy and ready for dipping. If at a party, it would be a good idea to get a hot plate to keep it warm so that it stays smooth all night. If it gets too thick, add a little more wine. Enjoy!

Fondue party, Anyone?

Easy Chocolate Fondue

- 1 package semi-sweet or milk chocolate chips
- 1/4 cup butter
- 1/4 cup of milk or cream
- Stuff for dipping (strawberries, pears, bananas, apples, Angel-food cake, pound cake cubes, Marshmallows, etc)

Start by gently melting the chocolate pieces, butter, and half of the milk on low heat in a sauce pan. Heat slowly, stirring constantly, over low heat until chocolate is melted and smooth. You can add 1 tablespoon of creamy peanut butter if you'd like to. It gives it a little more flavor. Cook and stir till heated through. Stir in additional milk, a little at a time, until it reaches the desired consistency. Be patient and go slow! If you burn the chocolate, you gotta start over. This will hold up well for about 1 hour on low in a mini crock pot or on a hot plate, bit if the fondue gets too thick, just add milk 1 tablespoon at a time.

Dip the night away! Have fun with your friends and enjoy!

Fondue party, Anyone?

(Mema's Chicken and Dumplings) - Dee - lish!!

Soups & Stews

Story Time: Shelley and I always loved going to Mema and Dedaddy's house. As children, we remember spending hours with Dedaddy in his workshop making "presents" for Mema. The gift was usually a very crooked stool-but she loved then all. After dark, we would play in the nursery until dinner time.

No matter how crooked those stools were, Mema would always ooooh! and aahhhh! over them and we would giggle with pride. We would play in the nursery until smells of dinner wafted to the back of the house and got our attention. We had a habit of sneaking to the kitchen to catch a peak at what Mema was doing and we always got caught. With a smile and a wink, Mema would send us back to the nursery. We could hardly wait to sit down with her and Dedaddy to enjoy her Chicken and Dumplings on our TV trays in the kitchen. This is one of my fondest memories of spending time with Mema and Dedaddy. even though the stools were probably made with the same pieces of wood. (I have a feeling Dedaddy would take the stools apart once we left so we could build them again the next time we came.

Lincoln Logs, Tinker Toys...

Mema's Chicken and Dumplings

- 1 chicken (cooked and de-boned without the skin - pickin' chicken ain't fun, but is totally worth it in this Southern Favorite!)
- 3 stalks of celery (finely chopped)
- 1 small onion (finely chopped)
- 1 small bag of frozen corn (not canned - it has too much sodium and sugar)
- 1 small bag of frozen peas and carrots (not canned - too much sodium and sugar)
- 2 tablespoons of flour
- 1 stick of butter
- 1 cup milk or cream (I usually use milk)
- 5 cups of chicken stock / broth
- 3 boiled eggs
- 1 package of pre-made dumplings (I don't have time to make my own, so I use Anne's Frozen dumplings in the frozen foods section at the supermarket with the frozen biscuits)

Fond Memories!

Mema's Chicken and Dumplings

Start by melting the butter in a sauce pan. Sauté the onion until it is translucent. Sprinkle in the flour. Let it cook for about a minute. Slowly add in the cream stirring constantly with a whisk until smooth. Now, add the remaining ingredients except for the eggs and dumplings. Shortcut: get a rotisserie chicken from the supermarket. Pickin' chicken ain't fun, but it's totally worth it! Simmer for about 20 - 30 minutes so that the flavors can really blend. Then, bring the mixture to a boil to add the dumplings (I like to take the frozen strips and break them into thirds so you end up with square dumplings). Drop the dumplings in one at a time so that they don't stick together. You also have to make sure that the liquid is boiling so that the dumplings actually cook. After the dumplings are in, drop the temp to a simmer. About 10 minutes before you are ready to serve, chop up the three boiled eggs and add them to the soup. This is when the 'magic' happens and you get the thick, delicious chicken and dumplings that we all remember when we stayed with Mema. If the dish is not as thick as you'd like, bring it back to a boil and add some corn starch to thicken it up.

Fond Memories !

Traditional Dumplings
(Just in case you have time)

- 2 Cups of All-purpose flour
- 1/2 teaspoon of Baking soda
- 1/2 teaspoon of Salt
- 3 tablespoons of Shortening
- 3/4 Cup Buttermilk

Combine the flour, baking soda and 1/2 teaspoon salt. "Cut" in the shortening with a pastry blender or two knives until mixture is consistency of coarse meal. Add the buttermilk, stirring just until dry ingredients are moistened. Turn dough out onto a floured surface and knead 4 or 5 times -- no more.

For rolled dumplings, roll the dough to a 1/4-inch thickness, and cut into 3" x 1" strips.

Drop dumplings, one or two at a time, into the boiling broth and reduce heat to medium-low. Stir from time to time to make sure the dumplings do not stick together. Cook the dumplings 8 to 10 minutes and serve. If you are in a pinch, you can use canned biscuit dough cut into quarters.

French Onion Soup

(compliments of Holly Williams)

- 1 and 1/2 pounds peeled onions (Yep...Pounds)
- 3 oz butter
- 1/2 cup green peppers (diced)
- 1 tablespoon paprika
- 1 bay leaf
- 1/2 cup flour
- 1 and 1/2 quarts beef broth / beef stock
- 1 cup white wine
- 1 and 1/2 teaspoons of salt

24 Hours in Advance: Slice onions and sauté on low - medium heat in melted butter with all the other ingredients except the beef stock. for *90 minutes* (yep! An hour and a half) Then add the beef stock and simmer for 2 additional hours. Now it's time to let the soup chill overnight.

When You are *Ready To Serve:* Remove the bay leaf and Re-Heat the soup and fill oven proof casserole dish (or oven proof bowls) with the soup. Top with 1/2 inch slice of French bread and Gruyere cheese (or Swiss). Set under the broiler until cheese is golden brown.

Thanks Holly!!

Crock Pot Stew

- 1 lb of cubed stew meat
- 1 can cream of celery soup
- 1 pkg of Onion soup mix

Combine the three ingredients in your crock pot and stir. Do not add any liquid. This combination of ingredients produces a savory gravy. Set your crock pot to medium/high for 4-6 hours. Serve over rice or noodles with a salad or another vegetable.

See, I told you it was easy!

Vegetarian Chili

- 2 Zucchini (diced and sautéd)
- 2 onions (diced and sautéd)
- 2-3 cloves crushed garlic
- 2 red bell peppers (diced)
- 1 large can of Italian tomatoes
- 1 and 1/2 pounds of ripe tomatoes (diced)
- 2 tablespoons of chili powder
- 1 tablespoon of Cumin
- 1 tablespoon Basil
- 1 tablespoon Oregano
- 1 teaspoons pepper, salt and fennel seeds
- 1/2 cup parsley

Cook the above ingredients for 30 minutes. Then add:

- 1 can kidney beans (drained)
- 1 can chick peas (drained)

Cook an additional 15 minutes and serve with a dollop of sour cream, Monterey Jack cheese or chopped scallions.

Yummy and Healthy!

Hearty Potato Soup

- 6 medium potatoes (peeled and cubed)
- 2 carrots (diced)
- 6 stalks of celery (diced)
- 1 quart of chicken or vegetable stock
- 6 tablespoons of butter
- 6 tablespoons of all purpose flour
- 1 teaspoon of salt
- 1 teaspoon of pepper
- 2 cups of milk of heavy cream

In a large kettle, cook the potatoes, carrots and celery in the broth until tender. Drain and save the liquid. Set the vegetables aside and sauté the onion in 1 tablespoon of butter until transparent / soft. Stir in the flour, salt and pepper. Gradually add the milk stirring constantly. Add 1 cup of the reserved broth and add the remaining vegetables. Keep adding the reserved broth until the desired thickness is reached. If there is any left over, save it in the freezer.

This is a very versatile soup recipe in that you can add cheese to make a chowder or you could add some broccoli or a little ham to make this any kind of soup you want.

Herbed Beef Stew

There are lots of ingredients to this recipe, but they each play an important role in the finished dish. This can be served over rice or straight up with French bread. You can omit the ingredients you don't like or add more of the ingredients you do like. This makes a huge amount of stew. You may need to cut it in half.

- 3 pounds of beef stew meat cut into 1 inch cubes
- 2 tablespoons of cooking oil
- 6 cups ob beef stock or vegetable stock
- 1 large onion (chopped)
- 2 teaspoons of pepper
- 1-2 teaspoons salt
- 2 teaspoons of garlic powder
- 1 teaspoon rosemary (crushed), dried oregano, basil, and marjoram
- 2 bay leaves
- 2 -6oz cans of tomato paste
- 2 cups peeled potatoes (cubed)
- 2 cups sliced carrots
- 1 large green bell pepper (chopped)-take out the seeds
- 1 package of frozen green beans or peas
- 1 package frozen corn
- 4 medium tomatoes

Brown the beef cubes in the oil. Add the broth, spices, paste, and all other ingredients. Simmer for 40 minutes or until the veggies are tender and serve.

Dee-lish!

Mandy's Brunswick Stew

- 3 pounds of ground chuck
- 1 whole cooked chicken (skinless and de-boned)
- 3 large cans of tomatoes
- 1 cup of catsup
- 1/2 cup barbecue sauce (hickory flavored)
- 1 medium onion (diced)
- Tabasco sauce (to taste)
- Salt and pepper (to taste)
- 2 packages frozen corn
- 1 can creamed corn
- 1 can of baby Lima Beans
- 1 small bag of frozen cubed okra

Brown the ground chuck, drain, and add to the pulled chicken. Add the rest of the ingredients (except for the corn) and simmer for 45 minutes. Then add the corn and simmer for 15 more minutes. Serve with saltine crackers or a couple slices of corn bread. It's great on a cold day sitting in front of the fireplace visiting with family and friends. It goes hand-in-hand with Bar-B-Que! Yummy!

Great with Bar-B-Que!

Great with Bar-B-Que

Hamburger Soup

- 1 medium onion (chopped)
- 3 tablespoons of butter
- 1 large can of tomatoes
- 3 cans of beef broth
- 4 celery stalks with the tops (chopped)
- 1 bay leaf
- 1 tablespoon of parsley
- 1/2 teaspoon thyme
- 1 teaspoon of pepper
- 1 teaspoon of salt

First, brown the hamburger meat, drain off the grease and set it aside. Sauté the onion in the butter on low heat until soft and transparent. Add ground beef back in. Now, add the tomatoes, beef broth, and the remaining ingredients. Cover and simmer over low heat for about 45 minutes. Remove the bay leaf and serve with rounds of cheese toast. You'll need to make alot 'cause everyone will want seconds!

Winter Days Cheddar Chowder

- 2 cups boiling water or vegetable stock
- 2 cups diced potatoes
- 1/2 cup diced carrots
- 1/2 cup diced celery
- 1/4 cup chopped onion
- 1 and 1/2 teaspoons salt (to taste)
- 1/4 teaspoon pepper (to taste)
- 1/4 cup margarine
- 1/4 cup flour
- 2 cups milk
- 2 cups shredded sharp cheddar cheese
- 1 cup cubed cooked ham

Cook the potatoes, carrots, celery, and onion in a large pot. Add salt and pepper to taste. Set it aside when done and don't drain off the liquid. In another pot, make a 'white sauce' with the margarine, flour and milk. Add the cheese slowly and stir until melted. Now, add the ham and vegetables. Add the vegetable stock until it is as thick as you want it. Spoon it up and enjoy in front of the fireplace with a good book and some good company.

Mexican Corn Bread

- 1 cup of yellow corn meal
- 1/3 cup all purpose flour
- 2 tablespoons of sugar
- 1 teaspoon of salt
- 2 teaspoons of baking powder
- 1/2 teaspoon of baking soda
- 2 eggs
- 1 cup of buttermilk
- 1/2 cup of vegetable oil
- 1 can cream corn
- 1/3 cup of chopped onion / scallions
- 1/2 cup of bell peppers (red, green, yellow-they all work)
- 1/2 cup of shredded cheddar cheese (white or yellow)
- 1/8 cup diced Jalapeno pepper (take out the seeds)

In a mixing bowl, combine the first 6 ingredients. In a separate bowl, combine the others. Now mix the wet and dry ingredients together. Stir only until moistened. Now, pour the batter into a greased 9-inch baking pan or a 10-inch cast iron skillet (I like using the skillet method - just be sure to heat up the skillet before adding the batter). Bake at 350 degrees for 30-40 minutes or until golden brown. Slice it up and enjoy. You can also use cornbread molds (they come in all shapes and sizes).

One of Jason's favorites....

Zucchini Bread

- 3 Eggs (beaten)
- 1 cup of oil
- 2 cups of sugar
- 2 cups grated Zucchini
- 1 Tablespoon of Vanilla extract
- 3 cups of all purpose flour
- 1 teaspoon of Baking Soda
- 1/2 teaspoon of Baking Powder
- 1 teaspoon Salt
- 1 teaspoon of Ground Cinnamon
- 1/2 Cup of chopped nuts (optional)

Pre-Heat your oven to 325 degrees Fahrenheit. Beat the eggs, then add the oil, sugar, zucchini, and vanilla. Then sift together your dry ingredients (flour, baking soda, baking powder, salt and cinnamon). Next, add the dry ingredients to the wet ones and mix together. Add your nuts. This is enough for 2 bread loaf pans. So spray your pans with non-stick cooking spray and add the batter. Bake for 55-60 minutes. This is a moist bread and can be served warm or cold. It freezes well too. So, you can eat one now and save one for later.

Just in time for tea?

Nanna Matti's Banana Bread

- 1 and 3/4 cup all purpose flour
- 2 teaspoons of baking powder
- 1/4 teaspoon of baking soda
- 1 teaspoon of salt
- 1/3 cup of shortening
- 2/3 cup of sugar
- 2 eggs (beaten)
- 1 cup mashed ripe bananas (3-4 bananas)

'Cream' together the shortening and the sugar (It is very important to do this first). Add the eggs one at a time. Stir in the freshly mashed bananas and add the flour, baking powder, baking soda, and salt (add it little by little ~ unless you want to clean flour off your counter for a week!). Place the batter in a greased bread pan and bake at 350 degrees for 45 minutes or until a knife stuck in the center of the bread comes out clean. We like to eat this one straight out of the oven. This bread freezes well and if you make a double batch, you can give one away or save one for later. Either way, it is dee-lish!

Thanks Nanna Matti!

Pumpkin Bread

- 1 and 3/4 cup of all-purpose flour
- 1 and 1/2 cup sugar
- 1 teaspoon of Baking Soda
- 1 teaspoon of Cinnamon
- 1 teaspoon of Nutmeg
- 1 teaspoon of All Spice (Optional)
- 1 teaspoon of Salt
- 1 egg (beaten)
- 1 cup of cooked pumpkin (canned pumpkin is a good shortcut to use for this one)
- 1/3 cup applesauce
- 1 cup of raisins
- 1 cup of chopped walnuts (or pecans)

Mix all the dry ingredients first, then add the others. Once mixed, add the nuts. Bake in a loaf pan at 350 degrees for 1 hour.

Again, this is a great recipe to double up on. Eat some now and save one for later. Or give one as a gift during the holidays (or any day for that matter). It's good all-year round.

Great for the Holidays!

Cranberry Bread

- 1 Package of White Cake Mix
- 1 Package of Vanilla Instant Pudding Mix
- 4 eggs (beaten)
- 1 cup of plain yogurt
- 1/2 cup of vegetable oil
- 1 can of whole berry cranberry sauce
- 1/2 cup chopped nuts (optional)

Pre-Heat your oven to 350 degrees Fahrenheit. Mix the dry ingredients together then add the eggs, yogurt and oil. Beat with your mixer for 3 minutes on high. Pour half of the batter in your loaf pan, then add a layer of the cranberry sauce. Now, add the rest of the batter and sprinkle with the nuts. Bake for an hour and enjoy. This freezes well too. So, make a double batch and give one away or save it for later. Yummy!

Cakes for Breakfast? Yep!

Salads & Sides

My Favorite Strawberry Walnut Salad

- 1 bag of baby spinach or baby arugula (or both)
- 1 pint of sliced strawberries
- 1 can of mandarin oranges (drained)
- 1 6oz. bag of walnuts
- 1/4 cup of gorgonzola blue cheese (or other mild blue cheese)
- balsamic or raspberry vinaigrette dressing (to taste)

This is the easiest salad EVER! Just throw all the ingredients into a salad bowl and mix together. Wait to add the dressing right before serving. Otherwise, you'll have a soggy salad before you're ready to eat. I wouldn't normally put all these flavors in one bowl, but once I tried it for the first time, I was hooked.

Add chicken, steak, or smoked salmon to dress this salad up a bit. Yummy!

Yummy salads!

Mandy's Curry Chicken Salad

- 1 whole chicken (cooked, skinned and de-boned)
- 2 stalks of celery (finely diced)
- 1 cup mayonnaise (or Miracle Whip)
- 2 teaspoons of yellow mustard
- 1 teaspoon salt and pepper (to taste)
- 1 tablespoon of curry
- 1/2 cup diced green or red seedless grapes (halved or quartered)
- 1/2 cup of celery (finely diced)
- 1/2 cup of yellow or red bell peppers (finely diced)

I know pickin' chicken ait't fun, but for the most part is much better than canned. However, if you are short on time, canned white chicken will work.

Mix everything together and chill for about an hour. Serve on croissants, crackers, mini pita pockets, or any kind of bread you want. It is delicious any way you serve it it!

Great for Sunday Brunch!

Savory Broccoli Salad

(Compliments of Grace Sarber)

- 1/2 stick of butter
- 1 package of Ramen Noodles
- 1 package of Lettuce or Baby Spinach
- 1 cup of broccoli tops and frozen peas
- 1 small onion (diced)
- Salt and Pepper to taste

Dressing:
- 1/2 cup of extra virgin olive oil,
- 1/2 cup of sugar,
- 1/2 cup of red wine vinegar.
- 2 tablespoons of soy sauce

Sauté the Ramen Noodles and the onion in the butter until soft. Then after it has cooled, add the spinach, broccoli, and peas.

Mix the dressing and refrigerate.

Add the dressing and croutons right before serving. Otherwise, you'll have soggy salad.

Thanks to Grace Sarber!

Grandma's Watergate Salad

- 9 oz whipped topping (I like Cool Whip)
- 1 can crushed pineapple (drained)
- 1/2 cup pecans or walnuts (optional)
- 1 box pistachio pudding mix
- 1 cup mini marshmallows
- 1 small can of fruit cocktail (well drained)

Mix all the ingredients except for the whipped topping. Once all the ingredients are mixed, then fold in the whipped topping.

Grandma's Waldorf Salad

- 1/2 cup chopped, slightly toasted walnuts
- 1/2 cup celery, thinly sliced or diced
- 1/2 cup red seedless grapes, sliced
- 1/4 cup of raisins
- 1 sweet apple, cored and chopped
- 3 Tablespoons of real mayonnaise
- 1 Tablespoon of fresh lemon juice

Mix the ingredients above, chill, and enjoy!

Thanks Grandma!

Crunchy Pea Salad

- 1 package (10oz) frozen peas, thawed
- 1 cup diced celery
- 1 cup chopped cauliflower
- 1/4 cup diced green onion
- 1 cup sour cream
- 1 cup Hidden Valley Ranch salad dressing
- 1/4 cup cashews

Combine all the ingredients, chill and serve. Top with chow mein noodles for a little extra crunch.

Mema's Cranberry Salad

- 1 can of whole cranberry sauce
- 1 package of strawberry Jello
- 1 cup of boiling water
- 1 teaspoon of lemon juice
- 1/2 cup chopped walnuts

Boil the water and add the gelatin, stirring until dissolved. Mix in the cranberry sauce, salt and lemon juice. Mema would pour this mixture into one of her kazillion Jello molds (usually the wreath) and chill.

Right before serving the cranberry sauce (usually with the Thanksgiving Turkey and dressing), she would invert the mold on a serving tray on a bed of lettuce and place it on the table with a spoon.

This was always the perfect compliment to any turkey dinner. You could always buy the cranberry sauce in a can, (you know.......the kind you have to slice), but with this being so easy, why would you want to?

Perfect at Thanksgiving...

Mom's Potato Salad

- 6-8 Idaho Russet Potatoes (you could also use the small red potatoes. They are a little sweeter-they're both good).
- 4 stalks of celery (diced)
- 2 tablespoons sweet pickle relish
- 4 eggs (boiled and peeled)
- 1 cup of Mayonnaise
- 1 tablespoon of yellow mustard (optional)

Peel and cube the potatoes. Cook the potatoes and eggs together until the potatoes are soft. Now, remove the eggs, drain the potatoes and let them cool completely. Now chop up the eggs, and add the relish, celery, mayo, mustard, and <u>gently</u> mix it together. You don't want to mash the cooked potatoes. This is great for picnics and parties. But remember, you need to be safe with all outdoor parties and dishes with Mayo. We could always count on Mom making her potato salad for pool parties. Deelish!

Great for picnics...

Easy Spinach Salad

- 1 bag of Baby Spinach
- 1 cup bacon bits
- 2 cups freshly sliced button mushrooms
- 1 finely sliced red onion
- 2 sliced boiled eggs
- Your favorite Italian Vinaigrette dressing

This is an easy salad.

...And VERY tasty.

Aunt Leese's Asparagus Casserole

- 1 large can of asparagus spears
- 2 cups crumbled Saltine Crackers
- 1/2 cup of butter (1 stick)
- 1 cup grated sharp cheddar cheese (1 small block)
- 1/2 cup chopped almonds
- 1 small can of cream of mushroom soup

Mix together the crackers and the cheese. Drain the asparagus and retain the juice. Mix the soup and butter together and add the juice from the can of asparagus. Now, layer the cracker/cheese mixture, asparagus, almonds, and soup. Keep layering until you either run out of stuff or until you run out of room. Top off the casserole with the last of the crackers and cheese. (OK...you can add extra cheese to make it extra tasty...)

This is the only way James will eat asparagus. It has been a holiday favorite in our family for as long as I can remember. Now, Shelley has the responsibility to bring the Asparagus Casserole if mom is too busy. We can always count on fights between Jason and the rest of us for the leftovers at Thanksgiving.

Woo Hoo! Enjoy!

Mandy's 5 Cheese Mac-N-Cheese

- 1 box of elbow pasta (cooked and drained)
- 2 cups of grated Cheddar cheese (white or yellow)
- 1 cup of Mozzarella cheese
- 1 cup of Monterey Jack cheese
- 1 small block of Velveeta
- 1/2 cup of Parmesan cheese (for a little extra zip)
- 8 eggs (beaten)
- 1 cup of sour cream
- 1 stick of melted butter
- 1 teaspoon of salt (to taste)
- 1/2 teaspoon of pepper (to taste)
- 1 cup of milk

Pre-heat your oven to 350 degrees. Cook the pasta until it is almost completely cooked (al dente). Now, add the remaining ingredients. It will look soupy, but have no fear. The pasta will absorb all the wonderful flavors and you will be left with the best Mac-N-Cheese ever! Once all the cheese is melted and everything is mixed together, pour the mixture in a casserole dish (or two-one for later), and bake for 50-60 minutes or until it is gooey and bubbly on top. Now add another 1/2 cup of cheddar on top and bake an additional 10 minutes. Let it cool a bit and enjoy!

One of my favorites!

Gigi's Sweet Potato Soufflé

- 3 cups mashed sweet potatoes
- 1/2 teaspoon of salt
- 2 eggs
- 1/2 stick of margarine
- 1 teaspoon of vanilla
- 1 cup of orange Marmalade
- 1/2 cup crushed pineapple and raisins

Now for the topping:

- 1 cup of brown sugar
- 1/2 stick of margarine
- 1/2 cup of flour
- 1 cup of chopped nuts (mom uses pecans)

Mix the top 6 ingredients above in a large bowl. Once thoroughly mixed, pour the mixture into a casserole dish and add the topping. Now, bake at 350 degrees for 30 minutes. Let it cool just a bit and enjoy. I have heard that some people use marshmallows instead of nuts, but then, it just wouldn't be Gigi's Sweet Potato Soufflé.

Great at Thanksgiving!

Main Dishes

Gigi's Lasagna

Sauce:
- 1 large can of diced tomatoes (or Italian tomatoes)
- 1 small can mushrooms (optional)
- 2 teaspoons each of Basil, Oregano, Salt, and Pepper
- 1 small onion finely diced
- 1/2 teaspoon minced garlic
- 2 pounds ground chuck (mom swears that using ground chuck is the secret)

Filling:
- 1 cup grated mozzarella cheese
- 1/2 cup grated parmesan cheese
- 1 large tub ricotta cheese
- 1 egg
- One box lasagna noodles

OK. Here we go... Brown the ground chuck and drain off the fat. Sauté your onion in the remaining fat left in the pan. Once the meat is cooked, add the remaining ingredients and simmer for 20 minutes. Cook the lasagna noodles per the instructions on the box. Add a little salt to the water because this is the only time you will have to season the noodles. Time to Layer: start with the sauce and cover the bottom of a 9 x 13 inch pan. then add a single layer of noodles. Now add 1/3 or your filling mixture. Add another layer of sauce, noodles and filling. Repeat until you either run out of room in your dish or you run out of stuff. Now bake at 350 degrees for 50 minutes. Then take out the lasagna and sprinkle the remaining mozzarella on top. Place the pan back in the oven until the cheese is melted or a golden brown. YUMMY! Thanks mom!!

Italian Delights

Shelley's Stuffed Shells

- 1 pound of Italian sausage (cooked and drained)
- 1 large onion (chopped)
- 1 package of frozen spinach (thawed and drained)
- 1 package of softened cream cheese
- 1 egg (beaten)
- 2 cups mozzarella cheese
- 2 cups of cheddar cheese
- 1/2 cup parmesan cheese
- 1 cup Ricotta cheese or small-curd cottage cheese
- 1/4 teaspoon of salt and pepper
- 1/8 ground cinnamon
- 10 Jumbo Pasta Shells (cooked and drained)

For the Sauce:
- 1 can tomato sauce
- 1 tablespoon minced onion and garlic
- 1 and 1/2 teaspoons of dried basil
- 1 and 1/2 teaspoons of dried parsley
- 1 teaspoon of sugar, oregano, salt and pepper

Mix the filling, stuff the shells, lay them in a baking dish, cover with your sauce and bake at 350 degrees for 40-45 minutes. Sprinkle with mozzarella cheese, Bake another few minutes until the cheese is melted, serve, and enjoy!!! Yummy!!!!

From the kitchen of Shelley Vignola...

Mom's Beef and Rice Pie

Filling:

- 2 cups minute rice (cooked)
- 1 and 1/2 cans of tomato sauce (mom likes Ragu)
- 1 and 1/2 cups grated cheddar cheese
- 1/2 teaspoon of salt and pepper (to taste)
- 2 pounds of ground chuck (cooked and drained)

Mom would serve this like a real 'pie' in a pie dish and everything. Very cool! So, here we go...

First of all, take the cooked and drained ground beef and line the bottom of your pie pan / dish. The hamburger will be the 'crust' of this pie.

Now, combine the minute rice, tomatoes, salt, pepper, water and half of the cheese in a bowl. Then, spoon the mixture into the hamburger pie shell. Cover and bake at 350 degrees for 30-45 minutes.

Sprinkle the rest of the cheese on top as soon as it comes out of the oven. Slice up your meat pie and enjoy! The first time I made this for James, he said "You're making what?..." But when he tasted it, he was amazed! Yummy!

James' Favorite Pot Roast

- 3-4 pound chuck roast or London Broil
- 3 Vidalia onions (or white onions- cut into quarters)
- 3-4 red potatoes (cut into quarters)
- 2-3 carrots (cut into 1 inch segments)
- 3 tablespoons or Worcestershire sauce
- 2 tablespoons of steak sauce
- 2 cans of beef stock or beef broth
- 1 package of beef stew mix
- 1 package of Onion soup mix
- Salt and pepper to taste

Combine the three ingredients in your crock pot and stir. Add just enough beef stock to cover the top of the roast. This combination of ingredients produces a savory gravy. Set your crock pot to low for 6-8 hours. Serve over rice or noodles with a salad or another vegetable. The key to tenderness is to cook the beef "low and slow"

See, I told you it was easy!

Crock Pot Dinners!

Turkey Tetrazini

- 2 cups cooked Turkey
- 1 can of cream of mushroom soup
- 1 - 4-oz can of sliced mushrooms
- salt and pepper to taste
- 1 cup shredded cheddar cheese
- 1 and 1/4 cups of Parmesan cheese

So...what do you do with all the leftover Thanksgiving turkey? This is one recipe that we use every year.

Blend 1 can of condensed cream of mushroom soup with the turkey, then add the sliced mushrooms (including the liquid), the cheddar cheese, 1 cup of the Parmesan cheese, salt, and pepper. OK, now you can add the cooked spaghetti / vermicelli. Then, pour the mixture in a buttered casserole dish. Top with the bread crumbs and the remaining 1/4 cup of Parmesan cheese. Heat until brown and bubbly at 375 degrees. (about 30 minutes).

You can also use this recipe with chicken. Yummy!

Thanks Gigi!

Easy Beef Stroganoff

- 2 tablespoons of vegetable oil
- 2 tablespoons pf All-Purpose flour
- 1 pound of top sirloin or tenderloin, cut into bite-sized pieces (stew beef works well)
- 1/3 cup chopped shallots (can substitute onions)
- 1/2 cup button mushrooms, sliced
- 1 clove of garlic (diced)
- 1 teaspoon of Salt (to taste)
- 1 teaspoon of Pepper (to taste)
- 1/2 teaspoon of chopped or dried parsley
- 1 cup of sour cream at room temperature
- 1/4 cup cooking sherry or white wine (optional)

Brown the beef cubes in the oil. Then sprinkle in the flour. Next add the shallots, mushrooms, garlic, salt, pepper, and nutmeg. Let all these ingredients simmer together until the onions are transparent and the mushrooms are soft. Then add the sherry/wine and simmer an additional 15 minutes (I usually don't add the sherry/wine). When ready to serve, add the parsley and sour cream. Stir well and serve over cooked egg noodles. Deelish!

James' Favorite

Grilled Pork Chops with Pear Chutney

- 4-6 pork chops (bone in or out - it all eats the same)
- 1/3 cup soy sauce
- 2 tablespoons of butter
- 5 tablespoons of brown sugar
- 1/2 Vidalia onion (chopped)
- 3 pears (peeled and diced)
- 1 teaspoon of cinnamon
- 2 tablespoons of Worcestershire sauce

Place the pork chops in a Zip-lock bag with the soy sauce and refrigerate overnight. When ready to grill, place the chops on the pre-heated grill (375 - 400 degrees) and turn after about 7 minutes (turn only once).

Now, for the pear chutney:
combine the onions and butter in a sauce pan and begin to slowly cook the onions until they are transparent. Now add the pears, brown sugar, cinnamon, and Worcestershire sauce and simmer over low heat for about 20-30 minutes or until it thickens.

When the pork chops are done, top them with this pear chutney and enjoy. (You could also use apples or peaches - any sweet fruit will work). Yummy!

The Perfect Prime Rib

- Prime Rib of Beef
- 5 tablespoons of cracked peppercorns
- 4 whole garlic cloves
- 4-6 red potatoes cut into 1-inch pieces
- 1 large onion cut into quarters
- 4 carrots cut into 2 inch pieces
- 1 can of beef broth

In a large roasting pan, place all the veggies (except the garlic) and one can of beef broth. Bake in a 425 degree oven for about 30 minutes.

Take your Prime Rib of beef and roll it in the cracked peppercorns until coated. Now, make 4 small incisions and insert the cloves of garlic.

After the veggies have baked for 1/2 hr, then place the prime rib on a rack standing up in the middle of the veggies and reduce the oven temperature to 325 degrees. Bake again until the internal temperature reads 150 degrees. To figure out the total cooking time, allow about 13-15 minutes per pound for rare and 17-20 minutes per pound for medium rare. Remove the roast from the heat and let it rest for 10 minutes before carving. Very Impressive!!

Easier than you think!

Southern Fried Chicken

- 4 eggs
- 1/3 cup of water
- 1/2 cup of Tabasco or Texas Pete Hot Sauce
- 2 cups of self rising flour
- 1 teaspoon of pepper
- 1 teaspoon of plain salt or garlic salt
- 1 teaspoon of onion powder
- oil for frying (peanut oil is my favorite)

Combine the eggs, water and hot sauce in one bowl. In another bowl, combine the remaining dry ingredients. Dip the chicken in the egg mixture and then coat in the flour mixture. Heat your oil to 350 degrees. Be careful not to overfill the pot with the oil (only fill it up half way). Now gently place the coated chicken in the hot oil. Always drop away from you to prevent splash injuries. White meat cooks in about 10 minutes and dark meat cooks in about 14 minutes depending on the size of the piece of chicken. You'll know it's ready when it is brown and crisp. Be patient. It will take some time. Don't add too many pieces to the pot. If the oil temp drops too much, the chicken won't cook.

Cool on a cooling rack or on paper towels. Keep warm in a 300 degree oven until you're ready to eat.

Mandy's Meatloaf

- 2 pounds of ground chuck
- 1/2 cup of tomato sauce or ketchup
- 2 tablespoons of Worcestershire sauce
- 1 sleeve of Ritz crackers
- 1/2 cup white onion (finely diced)
- 2 tablespoons of parmesan cheese
- 1/2 tablespoon of Celery salt
- 1 teaspoon of dried garlic

OK, easy, easy, easy....

Mix the above ingredients except for the tomato sauce / ketchup. Some people add an egg to bind everything together, but I don't. Feel free to add an egg if you want. It's time to get dirty...mix this with your hands. It just works better. Now, mold the hamburger into a loaf and place in a 375 degree oven for 55-60 minutes. When done, pour the tomato sauce over the top and bake an additional 10 minutes. Let it rest for a few minutes and slice it up. You could also make individual mini-loafs using a mini-loaf pan. It's fun to do individual loafs if you are serving for guests. Then they can serve up the sides themselves. Yum!

Trout Almandine (From S&S Cafeteria)

- Trout Fillet
- Chicken Mix (basically - flour, salt, & pepper)
- Saltine Crackers
- Sliced Almonds
- Batter for Fried Foods (1/3 water, 1/3 whole milk, 1/3 flour. Mix well together.)

It was always a tradition to go to S&S after church and S&S Cafeteria was kind enough to give me the recipe for one of our favorites! Enjoy!

With your hands, press the trout fillet in the chicken mix. Dip into the batter for fried foods. Place in a pan of crackers into which sliced almonds have been mixed. Press trout firmly into crushed crackers, fully coating the fillet. Fry in deep fat at 350 degrees for approximately 5 minutes.

Note: Do no put too many crackers in pan at one time. Too many crackers will result in crackers breaking up too small as trout is breaded.

An Old Family Favorite!

Sweet Dishes

Grandma's Chocolate Pound Cake

- 1/2 pound of butter (2 sticks)
- 1/4 pound of margarine (1 stick)
- 3 cups of sugar
- 5 eggs
- 1/2 teaspoon of baking powder
- 1/2 teaspoon of salt
- 4 tablespoons of Hershey's Cocoa
- 1 cup of sour cream
- 1 tablespoon of vanilla extract
- 3 cups of flour

Cream the butter, margarine and the sugar together until creamy. Add the eggs, 1 at a time and add the remaining 'wet' ingredients. Combine the 'dry ingredients in a separate bowl and add them to the wet mixture in batches. Be careful not to over-mix. Pour the mixture into a spring-form pan and bake at 325 degrees for 75-90 minutes.

Chocolate Icing: Combine these ingredients and frost the cake after it has cooled (completely cooled).

- 4 cups of Confectioners Sugar
- 1 tablespoon of solid shortening
- 1 teaspoon of vanilla extract
- 1 tablespoons of Hershey's Cocoa
- approx. 1/4 cup of milk

First Things First!

Aunt Leese's Christmas Cookies

- 3 cups of All Purpose flour
- 2 cups of granulated sugar
- 2 tablespoons of vanilla extract
- 4 eggs
- 1/2 cup of vegetable oil
- 1 bag of chocolate chips
- 2 tablespoons of butter (to melt the chips with)
- 1 teaspoon of baking powder
- 1 and 1/2 cups of powdered sugar (reserve 1/2 cup)
- 1/2 cup Hershey's cocoa powder (reserve it)

Melt the chocolate chips with the butter (you can do it in the microwave, but be careful that it doesn't burn. If that happens, you'll have to start over again). Mix all the ingredients into a mixing bowl, but when you add the eggs, add them one at a time. Not sure why, but it just turns out better. (I'm not smart enough to know why...sorry). The batter will be super thick. Now, refrigerate the batter for 1 hour. Then use a melon scoop to make little balls (depending on how big you want your cookies. Roll the balls in the remaining 1/2 cup of powdered sugar and Hershey's cocoa powder. Bake at 350 degrees for 12 minutes and let them cool. Cereal boxes are optional, but it just wouldn't be the same without them. YUMMY!

Almost Got It !!

Mema's Bread Pudding

- 10 slices of Cinnamon bread
- 3 eggs
- 1/2 cup of heavy cream
- 1 teaspoon of vanilla extract
- 1 teaspoon of nutmeg
- 1 teaspoon of All Spice

Combine the wet ingredients in a bowl. Cut the Cinnamon bread into cubes and place in a baking dish. Pour the egg mixture over the Cinnamon bread cubes and let it soak in the wet mixture. Now bake at 350 degrees for 45-50 minutes or until golden brown on top.

Father Frank's Shortbread Cookies
(with thanks to Pat Osteen)

- 2 sticks of butter
- 2/3 cup of sugar
- 2 cups of All-Purpose Flour
- 2 cups of milk

Mix the above ingredients. Roll out and cut with cookie cutters. Bake at 300-325 degrees for 15-20 minutes.

Easy Dump Cake

- 1 box of yellow cake mix
- 1 stick of butter
- 1 can of crushed pineapple (or any fruit pie filling)

OK...this recipe couldn't be any easier if I tried. All you do is literally DUMP the ingredients into a 9 x 13 greased baking dish and bake. No mixing involved.

First pour out the pineapple or fruit filling into the baking dish. Then add the cake mix on top. Now, slice the stick of butter into pats and lay them out on top.

Do Not Stir The Ingredients Together!

Bake at 350 degrees per the boxed cake directions. The moisture from the fruit filling and the butter will make this cake delicious!

Dirt Pudding

- 1 pound bag of OREO cookies
- 12 ounces of Cool Whip
- 1 stick of butter
- 11 ounces of cream cheese (softened)
- 1 cup of Confectioners Sugar
- 1- 3-oz box of vanilla pudding mix
- 3 cups of milk
- 1 teaspoon of vanilla

Make the vanilla pudding with the milk according to the directions on the box. Crush the OREO cookies into crumbs. Cream the butter, cream cheese, and Confectioners sugar together. Add the cookie crumbs, and vanilla pudding. Gently fold in the Cool Whip. Pour the mixture in a bowl and refrigerate.

To add a little flare, get a Terra Cotta pot and line it with tin foil. Pour the mixture into the pot and sprinkle the remaining cookie crumbs on top. Throw in some gummy worms and rolled out tootsie rolls. It looks really cool. hence the name...Dirt Pudding.

Thanks to Melissa Scites!

Mom's Banana Split Desert

- 2 cups of Graham Cracker Crumbs
- 1 and 1/2 cups of margarine (3 sticks)
- 4 cups of Confectioners Sugar
- 1 teaspoon of vanilla extract
- 4-5 bananas
- 1 can of crushed pineapple (drained)
- 2 containers of whipped topping
- 1/2 cup of chopped nuts
- 1 jar of maraschino cherries

Mix the graham cracker crumbs with 1 stick of margarine and press into a 9 X 13 baking dish. Mix the remaining margarine, sugar, vanilla, 1 container of whipped topping, and 1/2 of the pineapple for 10 minutes on high with your electric mixer. Spread the mixture over the graham cracker crust. Slice the bananas and place them on top of the creamed mixture. Cover the bananas with the remaining pineapple and "frost" with the other container of cool whip. Sprinkle on the nuts and cherries. Refrigerate and enjoy! This was David's favorite desert when we were growing up (next to Grandma's Chocolate pound cake - of course!)

David's Favorite!

Thanksgiving Pumpkin Pie

- 1 and 1/2 cups of cooked pumpkin (or 1 large can of Pumpkin)
- 1 cup of sugar
- 2 teaspoons of cinnamon
- 1/2 teaspoon of ground cloves
- 1/2 teaspoon of All Spice
- 1/2 teaspoon of Nutmeg
- 1/2 teaspoon of ginger
- 1/2 teaspoon of salt
- 2 eggs
- 1 tall can of evaporated milk

Blend the sugar, spices and salt together. Add the eggs, the evaporated milk, and the pumpkin. Pour the mixture into a 9 inch deep dish pie shell. Bake at 425 degrees for 15 minutes and then reduce the heat to 350 degrees and continue baking for about 45 minutes or until a knife inserted into the center comes out clean. Cool, serve with Cool Whip and Enjoy.

Mom's Ice Cream Cake

- 1 small bag of frozen raspberries
- 1 small bag of frozen strawberries
- 1 small bag of frozen peaches
- 2 gallons of vanilla ice cream (softened)
- 1 box of lime Raspberry Jello
- 1 box of strawberry Jello
- 1 box of orange Jello
- 1 angle food cake round (broken up into pieces)

This should be called the "OMG!" Ice Cream Cake. Why? Well, it's because you'll say "OMG!" when you taste it! You will need a spring form pan for this one. I've never seen mom use anything else. OK...Let's go: Pour the frozen strawberries in the mold first (keep them frozen). Now pour the strawberry jello mix on top. Now, add a nice layer of angel food cake. Next, add a layer of vanilla ice cream. Then, add the frozen peaches and orange jello mix. Add more angel food cake pieces and add another layer of ice cream. Now, add the frozen raspberries and raspberry jello mix. Next, add more angel food cake and add one last layer of vanilla ice cream and freeze. When you are ready to serve, Invert the mold on to a platter and watch as your guests start to drool.

Nanna Matti's Pink Astic Freeze

- 1 - 8 ounce package of cream cheese (softened)
- 2 tablespoons of Mayonnaise
- 1 tablespoons of sugar
- 1 large can of whole cranberry sauce
- 1 9-ounce can of crushed pineapple (drained)
- 1/2 cup of chopped walnuts or pecans
- 1 cup of cream whip or cool whip

Combine the above ingredients and pour into a loaf pan. Freeze until firm (usually overnight). Let thaw for 20 minutes before serving.

If you want to add a little extra somethin' - somethin', line the loaf pan with saran wrap and once frozen, invert the pan, remove the plastic wrap and frost with more cool whip or cream whip. Decorate with a few mint leaves and fresh fruit. Slice it up and enjoy!

Mandy's Wheaties Cookies

- 1 cup of shortening
- 1 and 1/2 cups of sugar
- 2 eggs
- 2 cups of flour
- 1 teaspoon of baking soda
- 1 teaspoon of baking powder
- 1/2 teaspoon of salt
- 2 cups of oats
- 1 cup of Wheaties cereal
- 1 cup of peanuts (optional)

Cream the shortening and the sugar together. Add the remaining ingredients and spoon the batter onto a cookie sheet. I like to use a melon scoop to keep all the cookies the same size. That way, they bake in the same amount of time and are more consistently cooked.

Yummy and healthy (as long as you don't eat them all in one sitting). Hee Hee Hee! Enjoy!!

Nanna Matti's Pepper Nuts

- 1 cup of Shortening
- 1 cup molasses
- 1 cup brown sugar
- 3/4 teaspoon of cloves
- 1 teaspoon of All Spice
- 1 teaspoon of salt
- 2 teaspoons of cinnamon
- 1 teaspoon of ginger
- 1/2 teaspoon of baking soda
- 3 cups of flour
- 1/2 cup sour milk (yep! That's what the recipe says - sour milk)

Mix the first three ingredients in a bowl, then add the remaining ingredients. Roll the batter into small balls (about peanut or almond sized) and bake on a lightly greased baking sheet for 15 minutes at 425 degrees.

Once they are cooled, they will get very crispy and crunchy. James swears that his Nana Shultz would store them in a pillowcase in the closet until Christmas. Not sure about that part, but we'll have to wait and see how it turns out.

Holiday Treats...

Easy Crème Brulee

- 1 cup of heavy cream
- 1/3 cup plus 2 tablespoons of granulated sugar
- 2 large or extra large egg yolks
- 1/2 teaspoon of vanilla extract

Preheat your oven to 300 degrees. In a saucepan over medium heat, combine cream and 2 tablespoons of sugar. Cook slowly stirring occasionally until small bubbles appear around the edges of the pan. In a separate bowl, beat the egg yolks and vanilla until smooth. slowly pour the cream mixture into the egg yolks a little bit at a time beating continuously (we don't want scrambled eggs here). Divide the mixture among four 4 ounce ramekins. Place the ramekins in a baking dish and fill the dish with boiling water about halfway up the side of the ramekins. Bake for about 30 minutes (or until the custard is set). Chill for 2 hours.

Sprinkle the remaining sugar evenly over the top of the cooled custards. With a kitchen torch, melt the sugar until it is golden brown. If you don't have a torch (I actually bought one - it came in a crème brulee kit), you can put the custards under your oven broiler until the sugar has carmelized. Serve with fresh berries or other fruit. YUM!!

The final touches...

www.ingramcontent.com/pod-product-compliance
Lightning Source LLC
Chambersburg PA
CBHW041541220426
43664CB00002B/23